CHANGING CLIMATES

WEATHER AND CLIMATE

CHANGING CLIMATES

Terry Jennings

First published 2005 by Evans Brothers Limited
2A Portman Mansions
Chiltern Street
London W1U 6NR

British Library Cataloguing in Publication Data
Jennings, Terry J.
Changing climates. - (Weather and climate)
1. Climatic changes - Juvenile literature
2. Climatology - Juvenile literature
I. Title
551.6

ISBN 0237527480

Designer: Giraffic Design
Editor: Mary-Jane Wilkins
Illustrator: Graham Rosewarne
Series consultant: Steve Watts

Picture acknowledgements
Ecoscene: page 2, 6 (left), 12, 15, 18, 20, 23, 24, 25 (top), 28, 31,
33, 36, 37, 39, 40, 43, 45
Terry Jennings: page 19, 30, 34
Oxford Scientific: front cover, page 6 (right), 9, 14, 26, 29, 35, 41
Science Photo Library: page 10, 17, 34, 41, 42, 44
Still Pictures: page 19, 27
Corbis: page 11, 25 (bottom)

Contents

Weather and climate

From earliest times, people have observed the weather because of its effect on their lives. In some parts of the world the weather is almost monotonous because it is so predictable. In other places, including the British Isles, northern Europe and much of the United States, the weather is always a subject of conversation because it is so unpredictable.

Weather patterns

If we look at the weather over many years, a pattern begins to emerge. In the British Isles, northern Europe, central North America and other places in the middle latitudes, summers are warm while winters are cold with ice and snow. There is about the same rainfall in June as in November. This pattern of typical weather averaged over many years makes up the climate of a region.

Although Antarctica and the Painted Desert in Utah, USA, have hugely different temperatures, they are both deserts. This is because they both have less than 250 mm of precipitation a year.

Climate variation

Climates vary enormously in different parts of the world. They are the biggest single factor in creating the environment in which we live. Climate affects the shape of the landscape and the plants and animals that live there, as well as the way of life of people and the homes they live in. Climate also determines the foods that we can grow or produce, controls the availability of drinking water and affects the diseases to which we are exposed. In regions near the Equator the climate is always hot and mostly wet. Deserts are dry, while the polar regions are cold with year-round ice and snow.

Why climates differ

Different world climates are caused partly by the Sun, which shines more strongly at the tropics than anywhere else, and partly by the way in which the Earth's atmosphere and oceans transfer heat away from the Equator to other parts of the Earth's surface. If the Earth had no atmosphere or oceans, it would have no climates.

Elements of climate

Both weather and climate are made up of the same elements: temperature, rainfall, wind, air pressure, humidity, cloud, sunshine, fog, mist, and many others. The two most important are average temperatures and average rainfall.

The Sun supplies the energy to power our weather. It also produces the energy to make water evaporate from oceans, seas and other moist surfaces all over the Earth. But to reach the Earth, the Sun's rays have to pass through the atmosphere.

The atmosphere

The atmosphere forms several distinct layers around the Earth. The outer layer gradually merges into the airless zone we call space. The lowest layer of the atmosphere is known as the troposphere. It rises above the Earth's surface for about 16 km over the Equator and about 8 km above the poles. The troposphere is the layer in which we, and all other forms of life, exist and it is also where all our weather occurs.

The air consists mainly of three gases: nitrogen, oxygen and argon in constant proportions. It also contains variable amounts of water vapour, and minute quantities of several gases, including carbon dioxide, neon, helium, krypton, xenon, methane and ozone. Altogether these other gases make up about 0.04 per cent of the atmosphere by volume. The air also contains dust, smoke and salt particles and plant pollen grains.

The Earth's atmosphere consists of a number of layers. Nearly all our weather forms in the troposphere, the layer closest to the Earth's surface. This is also where all life occurs.

LAYERS OF THE EARTH'S ATMOSPHERE

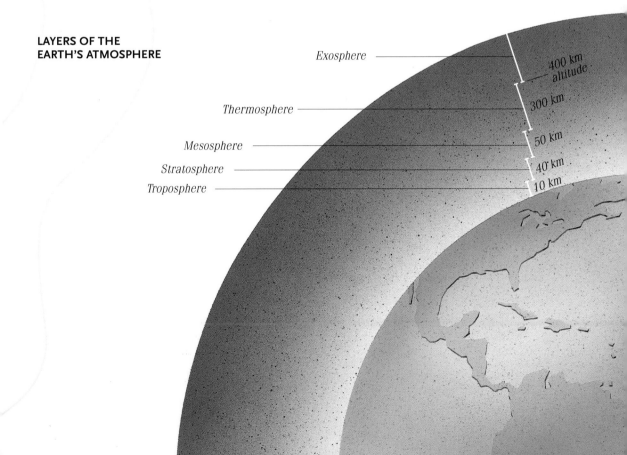

Exosphere — 400 km altitude

Thermosphere — 300 km

Mesosphere — 50 km

Stratosphere — 40 km

Troposphere — 10 km

WEATHER AND
BEHAVIOUR

*Weather can affect
behaviour. The föhn
wind, which blows from
the Alps into northern
Europe, brings sudden
changes in air pressure,
temperature and
humidity. It causes
headaches and insomnia,
and is said to affect some
people's mental health.
Most city riots have
started on hot, humid
nights. Lack of sunshine
in winter leads to SAD,
seasonal affective
disorder, which makes
some people depressed.*

Air pressure

On the surface of the Earth we are at the bottom of a sea of air. We may think that the air weighs nothing, but in fact it has substance and is many kilometres deep. An average classroom probably contains about 100 kg of air, while on every square centimetre of the Earth the atmosphere presses down with a force of about 1 kg. Air presses in all directions, not just down, which is why we are not squashed flat by it!

Air pressure varies from time to time and place to place. This is because of differences in the warming power of the Sun. When the air pressure is different in two places near each other, the difference creates wind. Wind is moving air that blows from an area of high pressure to one of low pressure until the two pressures have equalised.

Heat from the Sun

The Earth is a sphere, so the Sun heats the tropics more than the poles. The Sun's rays hit the area around the Equator full on and make it the hottest region on Earth. Near the poles the rays strike the Earth at a low angle and spread over a wide area, warming the Earth less.

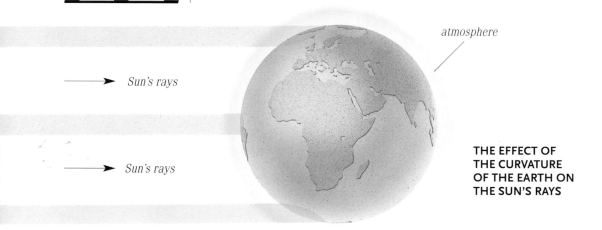

atmosphere

Sun's rays

Sun's rays

THE EFFECT OF THE CURVATURE OF THE EARTH ON THE SUN'S RAYS

Climate depends on how far a place is from the Equator. This distance, called latitude, is measured in degrees. The pattern is disrupted by three factors. First, the equatorial regions are often covered with cloud, which moderates the temperature. Second, large blocks of land heat up and cool down faster than the surrounding ocean. Third, temperature drops with altitude, so the highest mountains are covered with ice and snow throughout the year.

The importance of seasons

The weather changes regularly through the year. Places between the Equator and the poles (the middle latitudes) have four seasons. This is because the Earth is tilted on its axis and remains tilted as it circles the Sun. For part of the year the northern hemisphere tilts towards the Sun, giving that part of the world the long, warm days of summer.

On 21 March, the Sun is overhead at the Equator. All places have equal day and night. This is the vernal (spring) equinox in the northern hemisphere and the autumn equinox in the southern hemisphere.

On 21 December, the southern hemisphere tilts towards the Sun. This is the winter solstice (shortest day) in the northern hemisphere, and the summer solstice (longest day) in the southern hemisphere.

21 March

21 June

Sun

21 December

THE EARTH, THE SUN AND THE SEASONS

22 September

On 21 June, the northern hemisphere tilts towards the Sun. This is the summer solstice in the northern hemisphere and the winter solstice in the southern.

On 22 September, the Sun is overhead at the Equator. This is the autumn equinox in the northern hemisphere and the vernal equinox in the southern.

At the same time, the southern hemisphere is tilted away from the Sun and has the shorter, cooler days of winter. When the Earth travels round to the far side of the Sun, the southern hemisphere tilts towards the Sun and the seasons reverse.

Towards the Equator, places are less affected by the Earth's tilt so the climate is more constant. The seasons are not hot and cold although there may be rainy and dry seasons. At the poles there are only summer and winter seasons.

The shape of the land

The relief, or shape, of the landscape also affects climate. Warm, moist winds, forced to rise by a mountain range, lose their moisture as rain or snow on the windward side of the mountains. But when the winds blow down the sheltered (leeward) side of the mountain they become warmer as they descend and evaporate moisture from the land. Areas on the leeward side of mountains are often dry, or may be desert. They are in a rain shadow.

Mountain regions can also have lower temperatures than the surrounding lowland. This is because the Sun does not warm the air directly. Instead it heats the Earth, which then warms the air above it. As a result, the higher you go, the less the air is warmed. On average the temperature falls 2°C for every 300m you climb. This affects the plants that can grow on a mountain. It is also the reason why the tops of many high mountains, even those near the Equator, are covered in snow for all or most of the year.

The tree-line and snow-line on Mount Edith Cavell in Alberta, Canada. Their altitude depends on the distance from the Equator.

Land and sea

Oceans affect climate. Places near the sea have a milder and wetter climate than places further inland because sea water has a high heat capacity compared with land. When the Sun's rays strike the land, only a thin layer of soil and rock absorbs the heat. Over the oceans and seas the heat penetrates deeply and warms up a much greater volume. It takes a lot of heat energy to warm up an ocean, and once it is warm it takes a long time to cool down. By contrast, land warms up quickly but also loses heat quickly. So the temperatures of places near the sea are not as extreme as places far inland.

The differences between a maritime and a continental climate are shown by Edinburgh and Moscow, both a similar distance north of the Equator. The average maximum temperature in Edinburgh in January is 6°C and in July 18°C. By contrast the average maximum in Moscow is -9°C in January and 23°C in July. Moscow has extreme temperatures because it is far inland, but Edinburgh is close to the sea and has a moderate climate.

Ocean currents

Sea water is always moving. Warm water from the tropics flows towards the poles and cold water from the polar regions flows towards the Equator. Sometimes currents form a stream, such as the Gulf Stream. Most currents are caused by winds that blow in the same direction all the time, although some are caused by differences in salinity (saltiness). Currents can be altered by the Coriolis effect (the spinning of the Earth) and by coastlines. The result is a complicated pattern of ocean currents across the world.

The Gulf Stream is an important ocean current which begins with warm (26-29°C) water near the Equator in the Gulf of Mexico. This warm current flows up the east coast of the United States, across

A satellite photograph of the British Isles showing the temperature differences caused by the Gulf Stream and North Atlantic Drift. The warmest waters are red and yellow, and cooler waters are blue and green.

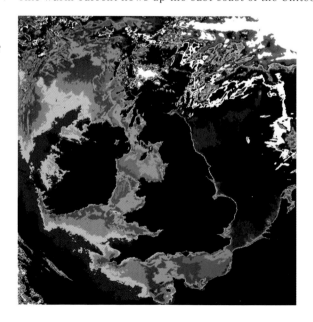

the Atlantic Ocean and fans out as the North Atlantic Drift. The warm air over the Gulf Stream and the North Atlantic Drift brings milder winters to parts of north-west Europe (including western France, the British Isles, Norway and Iceland) than you would expect so far north of the Equator. Without it, the seas around Scandinavia and northern Britain would freeze in winter. Cold currents, such as the Labrador Current, which flows south from the Arctic, have an opposite effect.

Grass and other plants grow on the Orkney Islands despite their northerly position off the north-east coast of Scotland. This is because of the warming effect of the North Atlantic Drift.

Warm winds

Winds blowing over warm ocean currents to land are also warmed. Because these winds are warmer they are moist and often bring rain. Winds blowing over cold currents, such as the Labrador Current, do not hold much moisture and so dry the land.

The effect of an ocean on the temperature becomes less the further away from it you go. The prevailing winds in the British Isles come from the south-west. They are formed over the Atlantic Ocean and warmed by the Gulf Stream and the North Atlantic Drift, so are warm in winter and cool in summer. They produce similar temperatures over the British Isles. The prevailing winds on the eastern coast of the United States also come from the south-west, but they originate over the North American continent. As a result, the eastern coast has hot summers, cold winters and a great annual range of temperature.

Land surfaces

Different land surfaces absorb the Sun's heat differently. Light-coloured surfaces, such as snow-covered land or sandy desert, reflect the Sun's rays, whereas dense forests and dark soils absorb them. Where a high proportion of the Sun's rays are reflected, clouds are less likely to form and there is less rainfall. Clouds also reflect the Sun's rays back into space, so reducing the amount of the Sun's energy reaching the Earth.

Changing weather patterns

The Earth's climate has changed many times since the Earth was first formed about 4.56 billion years ago. Sometimes the Earth has been much hotter than it is now, and at other times it has been very cold, with much of it covered by ice and snow during the Ice Ages.

Ice Ages

The term Ice Age is misleading, because during an Ice Age Earth is not always gripped by ice. Instead there are marked warmer and cooler periods. The cooler periods are known as glacials, and the warmer ones as interglacial periods. We are living in an interglacial period that is part of what geologists call the Great Ice Age. Altogether there have been 49 of these cold/warm swings within this Ice Age.

The last Ice Age

Tens of thousands of years ago our ancestors lived in a glacial period which lasted from about 114,000 to 10,000 years ago. Average temperatures were about 5°C lower than today and about a third of the Earth's surface was covered by ice. Ice sheets, in places more than 3 km thick, covered large parts of Europe, Scandinavia and North America. Huge glaciers flowed as far south as Berlin and New York, and icebergs were common in the Atlantic Ocean as far south as Portugal. So much water was frozen that global sea levels were more than 100m lower than today and people could walk from Russia to the United States, without getting wet feet. So early people could move from continent to continent in search of food or a better climate.

In the southern hemisphere, much of Argentina, New Zealand and parts of Australia and South Africa were covered by ice. Stone Age paintings in caves in the Sahara Desert show that it was grassland during the last Ice Age, and that lions, giraffes, elephants and hippopotamuses lived there.

The last interglacial period

Another 100,000 years earlier, before the start of the last glacial period, there was a warm interglacial period. At that time southern England had a subtropical climate. Elephants, hippopotamuses and cave lions roamed the countryside and their bones have been found in many places.

Ice floes in the Arctic Ocean, the smallest of the world's oceans. Scenes like this would have been common in the oceans and seas around much of Europe and North America during the last Ice Age.

TEMPERATURE VARIATIONS OVER THE LAST 200,000 YEARS

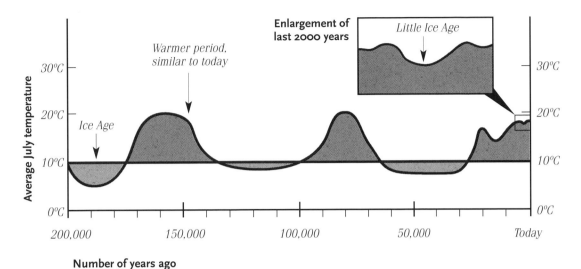

Number of years ago

The end of the Ice Age

The last Ice Age (or glacial period) started to end about 12,000 years ago. The Earth began to warm and the ice started to melt rapidly. As the sea levels rose, early people became more isolated from each other. Vast floods killed thousands of plant and animal species. By about 7,000 years ago, the coastlines of the continents had begun to take on their present shape. Although we are now living in a warm period, climatologists and historians have discovered that since the end of the last Ice Age there have been periods when it was warmer or cooler than it is today.

Recent changes to the climate

Scientists have been recording weather patterns and changes since the 1800s. Today they have many theories to explain changes to the world's climate. Recent studies have shown that major volcanic eruptions can cause cold weather. The volcanic dust blocks out sunlight and so cools the Earth. But volcanic eruptions cannot explain all climatic changes. Some scientists think that gradual changes in the Earth's orbit around the Sun or the tilt of its axis may have caused climatic changes. These may have resulted in the northern hemisphere receiving less of the Sun's heat than before, leading to the cold conditions. The fact that there are coal seams formed from tropical plants in Antarctica is the result of continental drift, the process by which land masses have moved and are still moving around the Earth.

Whatever their cause, these climatic changes were the result of natural causes. Today, our weather is changing because of human activities. The formation of acid rain and photochemical smog, the growing hole in the ozone layer and global warming, result from our pollution of the atmosphere by industrial processes and transport, which began during the Industrial Revolution and continues today.

WHOSE RAIN?

Rainfall has become so scarce in parts of China that scientists use guns, rockets and aircraft to fire dry ice or silver iodide crystals at cumulus clouds, to try to make them produce rain. The technique has become so widespread that it has sparked rows between neighbouring areas. In early 2004, the area around Pingdingshan in Henan province had 100 mm of rain, while neighbouring Zhoukou had just 30 mm. Officials in Zhoukou accused their counterparts in Pingdingshan of taking rain from clouds that belonged to them.

Natural changes to the climate

Although some climate change today is man-made, most is the result of natural causes. Some changes occur slowly as the Earth changes and develops. Others are more rapid and extreme.

Anak Krakatoa, a volcano in Indonesia, has erupted several times since 1928. Major volcanic eruptions have a big effect on the climate by pushing huge quantities of dust and gases into the atmosphere.

Early climate

Earth was formed about 4.56 billion years ago, when a cloud of dust and gas shrank under the pull of gravity. It had no atmosphere or water, and was as lifeless as the moon today. Slowly heat began to build up inside the Earth. Heavy materials such as iron and nickel sank into the Earth's core, while lighter materials drifted up towards the surface.

As the surface cooled, minerals began to crystallize, producing the first solid rocks. The Earth's rocky crust formed about 4.5 billion years ago. Volcanic eruptions produced vast layers of lava that spread across the Earth, and huge clouds of gas and water vapour were released. The lighter gases, such as hydrogen, drifted into space, while heavier ones were held in place by gravity. There they formed the first atmosphere.

The first clouds and rain

By about 4 billion years ago, the Earth had cooled enough to allow some water vapour to condense and form the first clouds. Eventually the first rains fell. Some rainstorms lasted for thousands of years and so much water fell that seas and oceans formed.

The Earth's first atmosphere had no oxygen. Most living things need oxygen to release the energy from their food. The Earth's early atmosphere was made up of unreactive gases. The first living things were formed in the oceans, around 3.5 billion years ago. The unreactive gases in the atmosphere probably protected early life forms and gave them a chance to survive. Later, when the first simple algae had evolved and begun to release oxygen, the atmosphere began to resemble today's atmosphere.

Volcanic eruptions

Throughout the Earth's long history there have been many volcanic eruptions, some of which affected the climate. Many eruptions pour huge quantities of sulphur dioxide into the air, together with vast amounts of dust and other debris. The dust can remain suspended in the atmosphere for years, while the sulphur dioxide forms tiny droplets of sulphuric acid high up. Both the dust and the sulphur dioxide act as a shield to block some of the Sun's energy.

The volcano Krakatoa was an island in Indonesia. When it erupted in August 1883, it caused the world's greatest explosion. The explosion, could be heard 5,000 km away and destroyed two-thirds of the island. Rocks were thrown 55 km into the air and clouds of dust caused darkness for days. For the next three years the dust scattered the Sun's rays and caused spectacular sunsets everywhere. All round the world there were cool summers and freezing winters.

When Mount Pinatubo erupted in 1991, satellites tracked the volcanic ash and gases thrown into the atmosphere. A month after the eruption, volcanic clouds had circled the Earth, blocking out sunlight. A fall in average temperatures of nearly 1°C was measured over a year.

This crater in Arizona, USA, was formed when a meteorite crashed into the Earth about 50,000 years ago. Large crashes shower the Earth with dust, affecting the climate over a wide area.

The impact of meteorites
Occasionally huge chunks of rock called meteorites strike the Earth. The impact of a large meteorite can send such huge quantities of dust into the atmosphere that the Sun's rays are blocked or scattered. As less of the Sun's energy reaches the Earth, temperatures drop.

Fossils show that dinosaurs lived on Earth for about 160 million years. Then, about 65 million years ago, they, and about 70 per cent of other species, disappeared. At this time, a meteorite 10 km in diameter struck the Gulf of Mexico, creating a huge crater. Lumps of molten rock showered North America and the Caribbean, and the blast set off huge fires and tidal waves. Rocks formed at that time show that the whole planet was showered in dust, which some scientists have suggested blocked the Sun's rays for months. The resulting cold and darkness prevented plants growing, and without plants to eat, millions of animal species died out. Whatever the cause of the extinction, it allowed the evolution of birds and mammals, including humans.

Mass extinctions

A mass extinction occurs when a large proportion of the Earth's wildlife is wiped out. There is evidence of at least six in the Earth's history. Nearly three-quarters of the world's species disappeared about 250 million years ago when movements of the Earth's crust caused the continents to form one giant landmass around a shallow sea. The Earth had been experiencing Ice Age conditions, but as the continents clustered together on the tropics, there was a fast rise in temperature. This mass extinction included 95 per cent of sea creatures, and probably had several causes, including climate change, a big drop in sea levels and huge volcanic eruptions.

The Earth's orbit

Changes to the Earth's orbit around the Sun and the tilt of its axis can also affect climate for hundreds of thousands of years and affect the timing of glacial and interglacial periods. The axis on which the Earth spins is tilted at 23.5°. About every 41,000 years that angle changes by a couple of degrees. Also, over about 100,000 years, the Earth's orbit around the Sun changes from being almost circular to an oval shape and back again. This alters the amount of sunlight reaching the Earth's surface, so that the climate begins to cool. Winters become longer, more snow falls, and shorter summers melt less snow.

Over thousands of years the accumulated snow turns into ice, forming ice sheets and glaciers. They reflect more sunlight away from the Earth, cooling the planet further. Only new changes to the Earth's orbit and the tilt of its axis can bring it out of this glacial period. But this isn't the whole story, and scientists believe that the amount of some gases in the atmosphere also makes a difference.

Moving plates

The Earth's crust is cracked, like the shell of a boiled egg, into 20 or more giant slabs, known as plates. The plates are not fixed, but slip and slide around the Earth by a few centimetres a year. The movement of the plates causes earthquakes, pushes up mountains and makes

CONTINENTAL DRIFT

About 220 million years ago the continents were joined together in one giant continent, called Pangaea. They have since drifted apart and are still moving today.

220 MILLION YEARS AGO

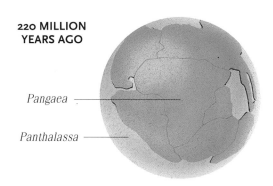

Pangaea

Panthalassa

200 MILLION YEARS AGO

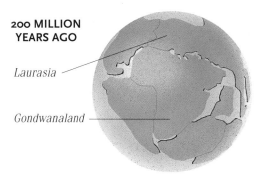

Laurasia

Gondwanaland

135 MILLION YEARS AGO

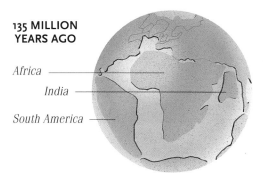

Africa

India

South America

10 MILLION YEARS AGO

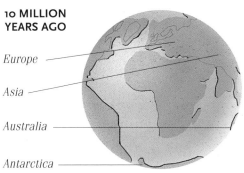

Europe

Asia

Australia

Antarctica

continents move. About 250 million years ago all the continents were joining together. They formed one supercontinent that geologists call Pangaea, which had warm climates because it lay on the tropics. About 190 million years ago Pangaea began to split into two parts: a northern section called Laurasia and a southern section called Gondwanaland. By about 100 million years ago, the plates carrying today's seven continents were beginning to separate. They slowly drifted to the positions they are in now.

In the distant past, many places had different climates because they were in a different position on the surface of the Earth. When Gondwanaland broke up, Africa was much further south, and so was much cooler than it is today, whereas Antarctica drifted towards the bitterly cold South Pole.

Sunspot activity

The Sun is a gigantic ball of hot, glowing gases. A million Earths could fit in its volume. The surface temperature of the Sun is about 5,530°C, and scientists believe that deep inside its temperature is about 15,000,000°C. The Sun's surface is always changing and dark patches, called sunspots, appear. About every 11 years the number of sunspots reaches a peak. Many sunspots mean that the Sun is hotter and more active, while few sunspots show that it is weaker and cooler. Some scientists believe that warm and cool weather and extremes of temperature may be linked to the sunspot cycle.

LINKED CONTINENTS

As Captain Scott and his party travelled to the South Pole in 1912, they puzzled over the coal, limestone and fossils they found in the Antarctic continent. Since then, many fossils have been found that link Antarctica with Africa and South America. A seed fern called Glossopteris has been found in Antarctica, South America, Africa and India. The fossil of a land reptile called Lystrosaurus has also been found on Antarctica and the other continents.

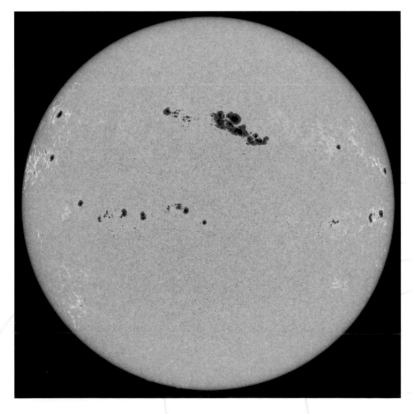

Sunspots reflect changes in the surface of the Sun. Many sunspots mean that the Sun is hotter and more active, while few sunspots mean it is weaker and cooler. Warm and cool weather and extremes of temperature may be linked to sunspots.

Studying past climates

Weather satellites and computers monitor our climate continuously, but scientists can only decide whether or not present-day conditions are normal by finding out what the climate was like in the past.

The Grand Canyon in North America was formed over millions of years. Layers of sediment, deposited by rivers and seas, gradually built up and were compressed into sandstone rock. Later the Colorado River cut into the rock, forming the canyon.

Information from rocks

Scientists rely on clues from rocks, plants, animal remains, ice and the landscape to find out about climate. By studying the layers, or strata, of sedimentary rocks, geologists can tell what the climate was like when they were formed. Sandstones and limestones are common in the British Isles, North America and other parts of the world. We know that sandstones were formed millions of years ago in ancient deserts, while limestones are largely composed of ancient corals and formed in warm, shallow, tropical seas. Coal forms over millions of years in hot, tropical swamps. Today there are coal seams in many cooler parts of the world, including northern Europe, North America and even Antarctica.

Fossils are the remains of plants and animals from the past that have been preserved in rock strata. They range from pollen grains to the skeletons of dinosaurs. The rock strata, and the fossils they contain, show some of the stages that the Earth's climate has gone through.

Between 570 and 245 million years ago there were cool seas, followed by deserts, tropical seas, tropical rainforests, and then deserts again. We now know that these changes were not the result of changes in global climates but were caused by the movement of the continents through the Earth's climatic zones.

The stories behind landforms

The shape of the landscape can tell us which places were once covered by ice. Glaciers carved out U-shaped valleys in the English Lake District and Scotland. Round lakes, called kettle lakes, such as those in Cape Cod in the US, Chile and Tibet, were formed when glaciers left behind blocks of ice. These were covered by rock debris which sank as the ice melted, creating lakes.

Glaciers often pick up large boulders (called erratics) and dump them in odd places when the ice melts. This large erratic on a Swiss mountain shows that a glacier once passed over the area.

Trees, sediments and pollen

Every year a tree adds a growth ring to its trunk. In warm, wet years the rings are wide, but during cold or dry years the tree grows little and the growth ring is narrow. By comparing the width of growth rings in ancient trees, scientists can find out about past weather.

Sediment is the soil and rock materials that build up in layers over time. A thin layer of sediments covers about 75 per cent of the world's land. They were deposited by oceans, rivers, ice or the wind. Scientists learn about past climates by studying them. Ocean sediments show how currents used to flow, while fossilized pollen in all types of sediment tells us where different plants have grown in the past. All flowering plants produce pollen; grasses and many trees produce vast quantities that spread widely. Every plant species has a different kind of pollen, and pollen grains can exist for many thousands of years without decaying.

Scientists in Antarctica drilling an ice core. The composition of the air bubbles trapped in the ice shows how the amounts of greenhouse gases have changed over thousands of years.

Ice cores

As ice forms, bubbles of air are trapped in it. Scientists use a drill to remove a long cylinder of ice, called a core, from a glacier or ice sheet. They analyse the chemical composition of the air bubbles whch were trapped thousands of years ago. Ice cores from the lowest layers of ice covering Antarctica contain air and dust trapped 400,000 years ago. By comparing the air and dust at different levels with those of today, scientists can see how the concentration of greenhouse gases has changed.

Global warming

In recent years, more and more scientists have found
evidence that the world's climate is becoming warmer.
They believe this global warming is due largely to the
pollution of the atmosphere by human activities.

*Drought in Tuscany,
Italy in 2003, when
the world average
temperature was the
second highest on
record. Examples of
this type of extreme
weather are becoming
more common.*

Record-breaking weather

One of the effects of global warming appears to be a succession of
record-breaking weather events and extreme weather. Data collected
from weather and climate stations, satellites, ships, buoys and floats
show that the 2003 world average temperature was the second
warmest recorded, although it was cooler than the record warm year
of 1998. The ten warmest years have all occurred since 1990.

During the past century, average temperatures at the Earth's
surface have increased by 0.6°C, but the trend has been three times
larger since 1976, with the high latitudes having some of the largest
temperature increases.

Heat waves and flooding

During 2003, temperatures were 1.7°C above average across large parts of Asia, Europe and the western United States. Warmer-than-average temperatures also affected much of South America, Australia, Canada and parts of Africa. In the eastern United States, western Asia, and coastal areas of Australia many areas had cooler-than-average temperatures. There was a record-breaking summer heatwave in Europe and France had its warmest summer on record. More than 14,000 French people died of heat-related causes in late July and August. Temperatures also soared across southern Asia in late May and June. During a 20-day heatwave, temperatures reached 45-50°C, and more than 1,500 people died in India.

Temperatures in north-western Russia were as low as -45°C in January 2003 and parts of the Baltic Sea began to freeze. Thousands of deaths were caused by extreme cold in India and Bangladesh during January. Snow fell during June in Moscow for the first time since 1963. In the Peruvian Highlands temperatures dropped below -20°C during July, and 200 people died. Santa Fe in Argentina had severe flooding after heavy rainfall in April and May. In South Korea heavy rains from typhoon Maemi in September triggered landslides and flooding, killing

130 people and forcing the evacuation of more than 25,000.

The extreme weather continued into 2004. In March a severe tropical cyclone named Monty swept across Western Australia. With winds blowing at 200 kph, it dumped 400 mm of rain on the Pilbara region, equivalent to four years' rainfall. Spring 2004 was the warmest spring on record in the United States, while the average global temperature was the fourth warmest since records began.

The human population

The Earth's atmosphere has served living things well for millions of years. Now the world is dominated by one species, Homo sapiens. People are so successful, from an evolutionary point of view, that now more than six billion of us share the planet. Within the next 50 years the human population could rise to more than nine billion. Teeming populations put pressure on the atmosphere and other parts of our planet's life support systems. A major concern is the accumulation of gases in the atmosphere from the fuels we burn. Burning carbon-based fossil fuels and wood gives off carbon dioxide, methane and nitrous oxide which are all greenhouse gases.

WHO CREATES CARBON DIOXIDE?

A quarter of the world's population living in the developed countries of the north produce about three-quarters of the world's carbon dioxide emissions and over half of greenhouse gases. The United States alone produces almost a quarter of the world's greenhouse gases. One US citizen produces as much greenhouse gas as 19 Indians, 30 Pakistanis or 269 Nepalese people.

THE CARBON CYCLE

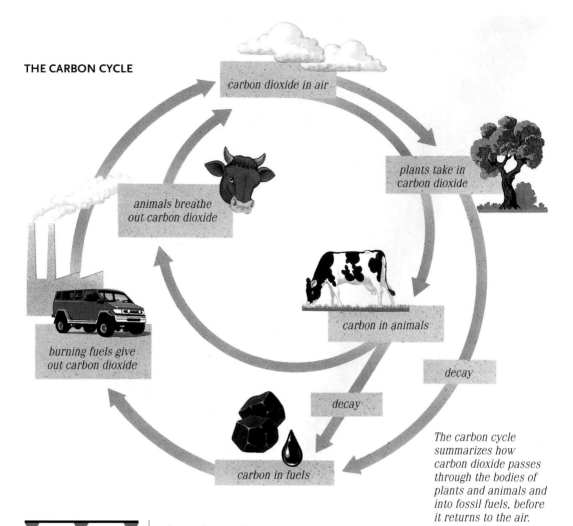

carbon dioxide in air

animals breathe out carbon dioxide

plants take in carbon dioxide

carbon in animals

burning fuels give out carbon dioxide

decay

decay

carbon in fuels

The carbon cycle summarizes how carbon dioxide passes through the bodies of plants and animals and into fossil fuels, before it returns to the air.

The carbon cycle

Carbon dioxide is one of the gases that make up the air we breathe. It is continuously created and destroyed and is part of a carbon cycle that includes all living organisms, the atmosphere, the oceans and the Earth's rocks. In the natural world, carbon is used over and over again.

Green plants are the only living things that can make their own food and they use carbon dioxide and water in photosynthesis. Plants take in carbon dioxide from the atmosphere and dissolved in surface water, particularly in the oceans. The oceans contain about 50 times more carbon dioxide than the atmosphere and act as a reservoir that helps to keep the amount of carbon dioxide in the air at 0.03 per cent.

The carbon in green plants is transferred to animals when they eat plants, or other animals that have fed on plants. Animals and plants release carbon back into the air in the form of carbon dioxide when they breathe out. When they die they decompose, slowly releasing carbon dioxide into the atmosphere. Plant and animal remains can form fossil fuels and their shells and skeletons can form limestone rocks.

Human activity can disrupt the carbon cycle. We release carbon dioxide that would have remained locked up for long periods by burning wood, coal, oil or natural gas. We also interfere with the removal of carbon from the atmosphere by destroying forests.

In 1987 an area of the Amazon rainforest the size of Britain was burned. This added 500 million tonnes of carbon dioxide to the atmosphere, and removed a vast number of trees that could have absorbed carbon dioxide.

Rising carbon dioxide levels

Carbon dioxide makes up only about 0.03 per cent of the atmosphere, but levels are rising. In an industrialized country such as the United States, more than a third of carbon dioxide released into the atmosphere is from fuels burned to generate electricity. Almost as much comes from vehicles and jet aircraft, and factories account for a quarter of the carbon dioxide. Central heating systems and domestic fires produce one tenth.

The greenhouse effect

Heat from the Sun is absorbed by the Earth's surface. Most is radiated away from the Earth, and some escapes back into space. Carbon dioxide and some other gases let the Sun's energy pass through to the Earth, but trap the heat coming back from its surface. By doing this, they act like the glass of a greenhouse and retain warmth. The Earth needs this greenhouse effect. If gases such as carbon dioxide did not absorb some heat, the world would be much colder. The oceans would freeze and the average temperature would be -18°C.

Until recently natural levels of carbon dioxide had kept the Earth at a comfortable average temperature of 15°C for thousands of years. Since the start of the Industrial Revolution we have built up a chemical blanket of carbon dioxide and other gases that act like extra-thick glass in a greenhouse, trapping more of the heat that used to escape from the Earth into space. So the global temperature has increased.

Clearing tropical rainforest by fire in Malaysia. This burning has a double impact on the environment. It releases carbon dioxide and also takes away trees that, alive, would remove carbon dioxide from the air.

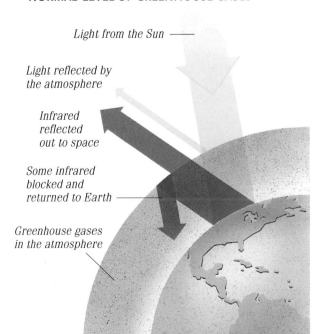

'NORMAL' LEVEL OF GREENHOUSE GASES

Light from the Sun ——

Light reflected by the atmosphere

Infrared reflected out to space

Some infrared blocked and returned to Earth ——

Greenhouse gases in the atmosphere

INCREASED GREENHOUSE GASES

Light from the Sun ——

Light reflected by the atmosphere

Less infrared reflected out to space

More infrared blocked by the atmosphere —

More greenhouse gases in the atmosphere —

Earth's surface warms up

Does more carbon dioxide matter?

Analysis of gas bubbles trapped in ice cores from Greenland shows that the level of greenhouse gases in the atmosphere has been linked to climate change for at least 500,000 years. When carbon dioxide levels increased, so did temperatures. Lower levels coincided with lower temperatures. Normally the carbon in coal, oil and natural gas stays locked in rocks for millions of years. But the Industrial Revolution changed that. We now pour about 6 billion tonnes of carbon dioxide into the atmosphere every year by burning coal, oil and natural gas. The gas bubbles in Greenland ice show that the amount of carbon dioxide in the air during the last Ice Age varied between 170 and 280 parts per million. Today levels of carbon dioxide are 370 parts per million.

A landfill site in Wales. When domestic rubbish rots, it releases methane, a powerful greenhouse gas, into the air.

Other greenhouse gases

As well as carbon dioxide, there are more than 30 other greenhouse gases. They include nitrous oxide, given out by fertilizers, vehicle exhausts, coal-fired power stations and burning rainforests. This gas can trap 270 times more heat than the same amount of carbon dioxide. Another greenhouse gas is methane, produced during coal mining and oil and natural gas production. Microbes in swamps and rice paddyfields produce methane. So do the digestive systems of cows, sheep and other plant-eaters, and decaying animal manure. Methane is released when we burn vegetation and fossil fuels and when we bury domestic waste where it can rot. In the last 200 years, amounts of methane in the atmosphere have doubled. Other greenhouse gases include CFCs and ozone, both described in Chapter 7.

The effects of global warming

The world average temperature has risen by more than 0.6°C since the middle of the nineteenth century. If estimates of the future build-up of greenhouse gases are correct, the average global temperature could rise by up to 3°C by 2050 and up to 5.8°C by the end of the century.

This may not sound much, but the last Ice Age was ended by a rise in temperature of 3-4°C. As temperatures rise, most climatologists believe the weather will continue to become more extreme. More water will evaporate from the oceans and seas, which will create more rain clouds and storms. There is evidence that we are experiencing more storms, hurricanes and tornadoes, but we do not know whether this is a long-term change. As precipitation and air pressure patterns shift, water may become scarcer where it is already in short supply and many low-lying parts of the world will suffer from flooding.

Melting ice

Almost four-fifths of all the fresh water on Earth is frozen solid in polar ice-sheets, icebergs, mountain glaciers and the snow and ice on mountain tops. The mass of floating ice over the Arctic is 5-7m thick. The vast Antarctic ice sheet has an average thickness of about 2,500m. In places it may be 4,000-4,500m thick.

Since the early twentieth century, most glaciers have retreated and their meltwater has helped to raise sea levels by several millimetres a year. The polar ice caps are also contracting. If global warming continues to melt the polar ice, sea levels will rise faster. Water, like everything else, expands as it heats up. So as the Earth becomes warmer, the water in the oceans will expand, raising sea levels further. They have risen by about 15 cm since 1880, and are likely to rise another 30 cm before the year 2030.

The highest point on the Maldive Islands in the Indian Ocean is only 2.4 metres above sea level. Even a slight melting of the polar ice could cause the Maldives to disappear.

Icebergs breaking off a glacier in Alaska, USA. All over the world glaciers are retreating as global temperatures rise.

The threat of flooding

The projected rise in sea levels of 30 cm by 2030 could affect about 200 million people worldwide. The United States would need to spend at least $450m more a year on flood prevention measures. For low-lying countries such as Bangladesh, the Netherlands and many island states in the Indian and Pacific Oceans, it could mean disaster. The danger is not simply from flooding, but from increased coastal erosion, higher storm tides, flooding from backed-up rivers and increased salinity in freshwater supplies.

Even more of a threat is the effect the warming of the oceans could have on the pattern of ocean currents. The top 2m of the world's oceans hold as much heat as the entire atmosphere, and ocean currents play a major part in transporting this heat energy around the world. Another unknown is what will happen to the multitudes of tiny plants and animals (phytoplankton and zooplankton) that live near the surface of the oceans and seas.

Global warming and agriculture

Scientists believe that global warming will raise the average temperature of the Earth by up to 3°C by 2050, but they cannot predict in detail what effect this will have on the world's climate. The higher temperatures may not be evenly spread. The rise will probably be higher at the poles than at the Equator, so the major crop-growing areas will move away from the Equator towards the poles. The main grain belt in the United States may move towards Canada and farmers will have to adapt to these changes. It will not be possible to grow some crop plants where they grow now and there will be a drop in yields in tropical and sub-tropical regions. As carbon dioxide encourages plant growth, crop yields may be higher in fertile areas.

A wheatfield in the North American grain belt. If global warming continues, the grain belt may move north towards Canada and farmers will have to adapt to growing new crops.

Global warming, wildlife and people

Human diseases, such as malaria and cholera, and deaths from heat stroke and skin cancer seem likely to increase. Some kinds of plants and animals, which are not able to adapt to the new climatic conditions, will become extinct. Those species particularly at risk are those very sensitive to changes in temperature.

In North America a butterfly known as Edith's checkerspot used to be common from Canada as far south as Mexico. The southernmost checkerspots are dying out, not because they cannot withstand the warmer conditions, but because the climate is too warm and dry for their normal food plants to survive. The checkerspots that live further north or at higher altitudes continue to thrive.

Until recently, the Dartford warbler was a rare bird that bred only in the most southerly counties of Britain. Even there, it risked starving to death in severe winters. Now the range of the Dartford warbler is spreading northwards because of the succession of milder and shorter winters.

One species that seems doomed if the sea ice continues to melt is the polar bear. Scientists estimate that one-fifth of the Arctic's summer sea ice could have melted by 2050. If that happens, polar bears will no longer be able to hunt, so will decline drastically. By contrast, it is possible that populations of pest species, such as rats, flies, mice and mosquitoes, whose numbers are normally reduced by cold winters, may rocket out of control.

One-fifth of the Arctic's summer sea ice could disappear by 2050. As sea ice is used by polar bears when they hunt, this ice loss could mean that polar bears become extinct.

Acid rain

Acid rain is another result of air pollution. The term describes the acidity not only of rain, but also of other precipitation, including hail, sleet, snow, mist, fog and dew. In recent years, acid precipitation has had a huge impact on natural and man-made environments across the world.

A coke plant in China. Air pollution in one country can affect the environment and people's health thousands of kilometres away.

The Industrial Revolution

Acid rain is not new. Complaints about the air quality in London were recorded as long ago as the thirteenth century, when coal was first used as a fuel in London. The Industrial Revolution made the problem worse, and it has been growing ever since. By the mid nineteenth century, thousands of coal fires had made city air so sooty that it turned buildings black and killed trees and other vegetation. Today, fewer people have coal fires in their homes, but there has been a vast increase in the number of power stations, cars, trucks, buses and aircraft, all burning fossil fuels and polluting the air.

The dead stumps of coniferous trees killed by acid rain in central Europe.

Fossil fuels and acid rain

Rainfall is always slightly acidic because carbon dioxide gas in the atmosphere dissolves in rainwater to form weak carbonic acid. When we burn fossil fuels, such as coal, oil and natural gas, this produces waste gases, including sulphur dioxide and oxides of nitrogen. Combined with moisture in the atmosphere, these produce sulphuric and nitric acids and make the rain even more acid.

Acid rain damages freshwater fisheries, lakes, streams, groundwater, forests, farm crops, buildings, statues, metal structures and human health. It is not just a local problem. Once acid gases reach the atmosphere, pollution may be carried thousands of kilometres, especially if the fumes come from tall chimneys. As a result, the acid rain produced by one country or continent can damage the environment of another.

Electricity and acid rain

Most homes in the developed world are powered mainly by electricity. It is easy to forget that, when we use electricity, we may be indirectly causing pollution. When we switch on a light, the bulb does not burn with a smoky flame, as a candle does. Neither do refrigerators, television sets and computers fill our homes with smoke. But most of our electricity is produced by burning. When coal, oil or natural gas are burned in a power station, sulphur dioxide and oxides of nitrogen find their way into the air, and these are among the main causes of acid rain.

Travelling pollution

Large areas of Canada, Scandinavia and central Europe suffer damage from acid rain because they are downwind of major industrial areas. Acid rain is also becoming a problem in Venezuela, the east coast of Brazil, parts of West Africa, central India, eastern China, South Korea, Japan, Malaysia, Indonesia and eastern Australia. Wherever there are large numbers of industries or vehicles there are signs of environmental damage from acid rain.

MEASURING ACID RAIN

Acid rain is measured using the pH scale, which goes from 0 to 14. The value of 0 is the most acidic, while 14 is the most alkaline. Pure water has a pH of 7 and is said to be neutral, meaning that it is neither acidic nor alkaline. Rainwater is always slightly acidic because it mixes naturally with carbon dioxide gas in the air. Unpolluted rainwater has a pH value of about 5.5. Vinegar has a pH value of 2.2 and lemon juice 2.3. Today, the most acidic rain falling in the United States has a pH of about 4.3.

A stone carving eroded by acid rain in Cambridgeshire, England.

BURNING OIL WELLS

At the end of the Gulf War in 1991, Iraqi troops set alight many of the oil wells in Kuwait. This released huge quantities of sulphur dioxide and other pollutants into the atmosphere. The acid pollution was spread when it rained and when water was used to control the fires. As a result of the acid rain, the people of Kuwait suffered high levels of asthma, colds, burning eyes and sore throats. The acid rain also damaged buildings.

Record-breaking acid rain

One of the highest concentrations of acid rain in the world falls on the state of Pennsylvania in the United States. Pennsylvania is a coal, oil and iron mining centre. Its industries include the production of steel, machinery, electrical equipment and chemicals. Recent studies of the rainfall in Pennsylvania show that it is nearly one thousand times the acidity of pure water. When this acid rain enters the lakes and rivers it has a devastating effect on aquatic wildlife.

Acid rain and rocks

If acid rain falls where rocks and soils are alkaline, such as in chalk and limestone areas, the acid is neutralized and there is very little damage to the environment. If it falls where the rocks and soils are already acid, for example in areas where the underlying rock is granite, the acid is not neutralized and the damage can be severe.

The effect on lakes and rivers

The effects of acid rain are most obvious in aquatic habitats. The rain runs off the land into lakes, rivers, streams and marshes, as well as falling directly on them. As the water acidity increases, the numbers of fish and other animals that can live in it begin to drop.

Some species of plant and animal are better able to survive in acidic waters than others. Freshwater shrimps, mussels and water snails are the first to die, followed by fish such as salmon, roach and minnows. The eggs and young of the fish are worst affected, and acid water can prevent fish eggs from hatching or deform the young fish. The acidity of the water also affects plants and animals indirectly because it causes toxic substances such as aluminium to be released into the water from the soil, harming fish and other aquatic animals.

Lakes, rivers, streams and marshes have fragile ecosystems, with all the species linked by complex food chains. So the loss of one species through acid pollution can upset the natural balance, leading to the loss of some species and unnaturally large populations of others.

Forestry and agriculture

Acid rain reduces crop yields and destroys trees because it washes essential plant foods from the soil. This makes sensitive trees and other plants grow more slowly or even kills them. In addition, the acid rain washes the protective waxy coating off plant leaves, leaving them more vulnerable to drought or attack from pests and diseases. Many of Europe and North America's great forests have been damaged by acid rain. There has been widespread damage in forests in the north-eastern United States and Canada and as much as 70 per cent of Germany's Black Forest has been damaged.

Acid rain and the built environment

Acid rain also corrodes, or wears away, the outer surfaces of stone buildings, statues and monuments, as well as paintwork on vehicles and buildings, and metal structures such as steel bridges and railings.

Many of the world's great monuments, churches, cathedrals and famous statues show signs of damage by acid rain, from Michelangelo's statue of David and the Parthenon, to the stone monuments on the battleground at Gettysburg and the Taj Mahal in India,

The effects on human health

Acid rain also affects human health. Most of the damage is to the respiratory system. Sulphuric and nitric acids in acid rain cause asthma, dry coughs, headaches, and eye, nose and throat problems. Toxic metals dissolved by the acid rain can enter the human food chain when they are absorbed by fruits and vegetables or are passed on to the animals from which we obtain meat, milk and eggs. Aluminium, for example, which is leached from the soil by acid rain, causes kidney problems and has been linked to Alzheimer's disease.

Smoke and fog

Some of the gases that pollute the air, such as CFCs, are invisible. Others, especially exhaust fumes from vehicle exhausts and smoke from factory chimneys, carry tiny particles. When there is fog in cities and industrial areas, these particles of solid matter, especially those from smoke, are trapped in the atmosphere. The resulting mixture of smoke and fog is known as smog. This form of air pollution affects human health, buildings, animals and plants.

Smog, caused mainly by vehicle exhaust fumes, hangs over Hong Kong, China.

Smog is not a recent problem. As long ago as the thirteenth century, the government investigated the problems of smoke pollution in London, and in 1620, King James I complained that smoke and soot were soiling St Paul's Cathedral. The word smog was first used in 1905 by H.A. Des Voeux to describe the atmospheric conditions above many British towns and cities. Des Voeux estimated that more than 1,000 people had died in 1909 in the Scottish cities of Glasgow and Edinburgh because of illnesses brought on or made worse by smog.

London smog

In persistent smogs so much soot may accumulate in the fog that it is dangerous to breathe it. In December 1952, smog covered London and killed about 4,000 people. This type of smog is now rare in London because coal burning was banned in 1956. Smokeless zones were created and the smoke emitted by factories and power stations controlled. But this does not happen everywhere.

Every year factories in Benxi, an industrial city near China's border with North Korea, produce 87 million cubic metres of polluting gases and 213,000 tonnes of smoke and dust. This atmospheric pollution makes Benxi invisible from satellites in space.

Pollution from vehicles

In the worst kind of smog, visibility is often reduced to 4m or less. Today there is still smog hanging over London, but it is less visible than it used to be. This newer and serious problem is the special kind of smog produced by vehicle exhausts. Under some conditions, the exhaust gases given off by vehicles may not be able to escape into the upper atmosphere. Instead they hang in the air about 900m above ground. They then produce a severe form of air pollution that contains such poisonous chemicals as carbon monoxide, ozone, nitrogen dioxide, benzine and aldehydes. This cocktail of pollution can cause asthma, bronchitis and eye complaints.

The fact that London has a cloudy and breezy climate means that the smog does not linger for very long. Cities in sunnier parts of the world, where the air is often calm, are at much greater risk. Los Angeles in the United States and Mexico City are famous for their smog, as are Bangkok in Thailand, Jakarta in Indonesia and many other expanding cities in the developing world. Even relatively small cities, such as Granada in southern Spain, suffer from smog.

ACID RAIN IN HISTORY

In June 1783 a volcano on Iceland erupted. By October the lava covered 600 sq km. No-one was killed by the lava flows, but the fine ash from the volcano stunted the growth of the summer grazing lands, while the sulphur dioxide in the gases it gave off dissolved in rainwater, producing sulphuric acid. This poisoned animals, fish catches dropped, and a famine killed more than 9,000 people. There was extreme weather over Europe, North America, Asia and Japan. In July 1783 there was snow in Poland and Russsia, and frost and high rainfall ruined the rice harvest in Japan. The acid and dust lingered in the lower stratosphere for a year or more and the winters of 1784, 1785 and 1786 were some of the coldest of the century.

Photochemical smog

Mexico City, Los Angeles and Granada suffer from smog because they are surrounded by hills. They are in low rainfall areas and regularly experience the warm, clear, calm conditions that are perfect for the formation of smog. The fumes rise from the huge amount of traffic, as well as from factories and oil refineries.

From time to time, a layer of warm air, often associated with a high-pressure system, then acts like a lid, trapping the cooler, polluted air below. Meanwhile, the sunlight changes the fumes into damaging ozone and choking smog. This layer remains trapped, stretching from the ground up to 150-300m, sometimes for several days at a time. This type of pollution is called photochemical smog. The situation in Mexico City is so bad that breathing the air there is said to be as harmful as smoking 40 cigarettes a day.

As well as being a threat to human health, the toxic gases in smog and pollution haze cause significant damage to plants, including plants which are grown as crops. In southern California, for example, desert plants that originally evolved to survive in

Los Angeles suffers from photochemical smog because exhaust fumes from the large number of vehicles are trapped by the surrounding hills.

pure, clean air are now suffering damage as a result of the air pollution which comes from Los Angeles and San Diego.

Asian Brown Haze
In recent years a brownish-coloured haze has affected much of India and South-East Asia. Called Asian Brown Haze, this type of air pollution is caused by fumes from traffic, power stations and factories and the smoke from fires used to clear forest areas for farmland. This form of air pollution again leads to a huge increase in the numbers of people with lung infections and breathing problems such as asthma and bronchitis.

A traffic policeman wears a mask to protect himself from the smog in Bangkok, Thailand.

LICHENS AT RISK

A lichen is not one living organism but two – a fungus and an alga. Neither can survive alone. The fungus provides a base for the alga to grow on, and soaks up water and mineral salts. The alga, like all green plants, uses sunlight to help make food for itself and the fungus. Lichens grow slowly, but can live where other plants cannot, including on tree bark, rock surfaces, bare brick and even concrete. But they are very sensitive to air pollution. During the nineteenth and much of the twentieth century, lichens began to disappear in urban areas of Europe and the United States because they could not tolerate the sulphur dioxide created by burning coal. In some places they are now making a recovery, because the amount of sulphur dioxide in the air has fallen.

Reducing acid rain

In Norway and Sweden, and to a lesser extent in the United States, the problem of acid rain is being tackled by adding lime to lakes and streams to neutralise the acid. The treatment works, but it is only temporary. It is also expensive and has to be repeated every three to five years.

Most of the gases that produce acid rain probably come from power stations and factories. Vehicle exhaust fumes also contain acid gases. Power stations and factory chimneys can be fitted with devices that remove the sulphur dioxide gas, while cars can be fitted with catalytic converters, which reduce the nitrogen oxides in exhaust fumes.

Burning fossil fuels is still one of the cheapest ways of producing electricity, so scientists are researching new ways to burn these fuels without producing so much pollution. Hydroelectric and nuclear power are alternative ways of producing electricity. They do not produce acid rain, but they do affect the environment in other ways. Solar power and wind turbines also produce electricity without pollution, but they are not reliable when it is not sunny or windy. There are also alternative sources of energy for vehicles, including battery power, liquid gas and fuel cells but they are not yet widely used. There is more about the possible solutions to global warming, acid rain and other environmental pollution problems in Chapter 10.

Wind turbines, such as these in Alberta, Canada, produce electricity from a sustainable source without polluting the atmosphere.

CFCs and the ozone layer

7

Oxygen makes up about one-fifth of the air we breathe and is essential to us and almost all other forms of life. Ozone is a form of oxygen present in very small amounts in the atmosphere. It can be helpful or harmful to the climate and living things, depending on where it is.

Ozone – friend and foe

Ozone is a toxic gas which exists throughout the atmosphere. Near the ground, ozone in smog is harmful to humans and other living things. Ozone is also an important greenhouse gas. The highest concentrations of ozone are in the stratosphere, about 20 to 25 km above the Earth's surface. Here, it is continually formed from oxygen, and it turns back into oxygen when it breaks down.

This layer of ozone shields the Earth's surface against ultraviolet radiation from the Sun. Ultraviolet is one of many kinds of waves and rays emitted by the Sun, which include the light green plants need to grow, and the heat that warms us. Too much ultraviolet radiation is harmful, not only to people and other animals, but to plants as well, because it can damage or kill cells. Ozone absorbs the ultraviolet radiation from the Sun and re-emits its energy as heat.

The hole in the ozone layer

For millions of years the protective layer of ozone around the Earth was stable. Then in 1985, Joe Farman of the British Antarctic Survey discovered that the ozone layer over the Antarctic thins to a minimum thickness between September and November every year. The 'hole' is about the size of the United States and as deep as Mount Everest. A similar, but smaller, hole in the ozone layer has since been found over the North Pole, and there is also a general thinning of the ozone layer over the rest of the world. As a result more ultraviolet radiation from the Sun now reaches the Earth.

The Antarctic ozone hole forms during the southern winter and reaches a maximum each spring. The thinnest part of the ozone layer is shown in dark blue.

What causes the damage?

Scientists studying the ozone holes believe they are caused by a group of chemicals known as chlorofluorocarbons, or CFCs. CFCs have no smell or colour, do not burn or react with other chemicals, and are completely non-toxic. For many years after CFCs were discovered in 1930, they were used as propellants to force out the contents of aerosol cans as a fine spray. Most aerosols now use other propellants. CFCs were also used in refrigeration and air-conditioning units, dry cleaning, and the plastic foam used to make hamburger and egg cartons.

CFCs and global warming

CFCs rise from the Earth and accumulate in the stratosphere. There the Sun's ultraviolet light breaks them down, releasing chlorine atoms. The chlorine attacks the ozone. One chlorine atom can destroy 100,000 ozone molecules. As the chlorine from CFCs destroys the ozone, more ultraviolet rays from the Sun reach the Earth's surface.

We now know that CFCs also contribute to global warming. One molecule of the most common type of CFC contributes ten thousand times as much to global warming as one molecule of carbon dioxide. Carbon dioxide is considered the most important greenhouse gas, but this is only because it is much more common.

The Montreal Protocol

In 1987, the United Nations held a conference in Montreal, Canada, to look at controlling CFCs. It agreed that the major user countries would phase out CFCs by 2000. Developing countries, such as China and India, can continue using them until 2010. But there are no natural mechanisms to remove CFCs from the atmosphere. Even if we stopped producing them today, it might be 50 years before the ozone layer repairs itself.

Ultraviolet light and human health

The thinner ozone layer gives the Earth less protection from the Sun's ultraviolet rays. As more reach the Earth more people are likely to suffer from skin cancer and eye cataracts. This has already happened near the Arctic and Antarctic. If the ozone holes grow, these problems could affect millions of people around the world.

OZONE-MAKERS

Ozone can be dangerous when it is near the ground. It is created naturally by lightning discharges. It is also formed by electric motors and any other machinery that creates electric sparks, as well as by exhaust gases from engines. These can form ozone when they react with sunlight. In areas with dense traffic, these reactions can raise the ozone content of the air to ten times its normal level.

Refrigerators being recycled in south-east England. Safe disposal of refrigerators and freezers is essential to prevent CFCs escaping into the atmosphere.

8

El Niño

Oceans affect weather and climate, and none more so than the Pacific Ocean. Here, a current of warm water which usually flows west changes direction every two to seven years, causing climate change in many parts of the world.

An El Niño event

During an El Niño event the western Americas have heavier rainfall and more floods than usual, while South-East Asia, Australia and Africa have less rain. Normally the trade winds that blow from east to west across the equatorial part of the Pacific Ocean push water warmed by the tropical Sun west. So the waters on the western side of the Pacific may be more than 10°C warmer than those on the eastern side. Over warm water, air pressure is low and lighter, moist air rises and brings heavy rain to South-East Asia, New Guinea and northern Australia. On the eastern side of the Pacific, where the water is cold, air pressure is high and there is little rain along the western coasts of South America.

When the ocean current reverses during an El Niño event, the cold area in the eastern Pacific and the warm western area swap. The pressure reverses and the trade winds weaken or reverse direction. The warm water moves east along the Equator towards the South American coast, where it spreads north and south. On the western side of the Pacific, no rain falls and Australia, Indonesia and

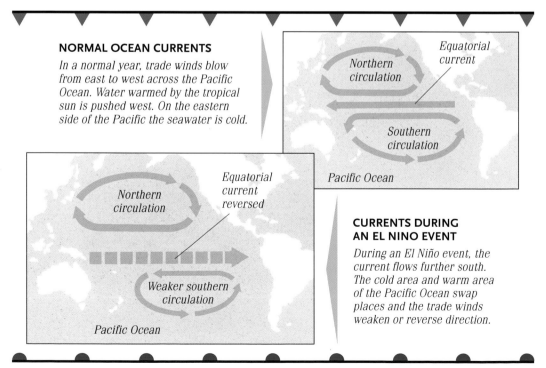

NORMAL OCEAN CURRENTS

In a normal year, trade winds blow from east to west across the Pacific Ocean. Water warmed by the tropical sun is pushed west. On the eastern side of the Pacific the seawater is cold.

Northern circulation

Equatorial current

Southern circulation

Pacific Ocean

Northern circulation

Equatorial current reversed

Weaker southern circulation

Pacific Ocean

CURRENTS DURING AN EL NINO EVENT

During an El Niño event, the current flows further south. The cold area and warm area of the Pacific Ocean swap places and the trade winds weaken or reverse direction.

Borneo suffer drought. There are droughts, and reduced crop yields too, in India and in the Sahel, southern Africa and Brazil.

An El Niño event changes the temperature of the ocean, which causes changes in the atmosphere. The warm surface water heats the air above, creating storms, typhoons and hurricanes. Some places have drought, and northern Peru, Ecuador, and California in the USA, have increased rain. The mass of warm surface water along the coast of South America prevents cold, nutrient-rich water rising to the surface. There is less food for the fish, which die or migrate in search of food. Fishery catches drop, and many sea creatures die of starvation.

La Niña
An El Niño event is often followed by unusual cooling on the eastern side of the Pacific Ocean called La Niña. Extra-strong winds push more warm surface water than usual west towards Indonesia. Around the Americas, cold, deep-sea water rises to fill the space. Less water evaporates from this so storms are less frequent here, but more frequent over the warm waters in the western Pacific. The 1988-89 La Niña event began a seven-year drought in California, while further up the coastline, the Pacific north-west had heavy rains and flooding.

El Niño and climate change
Some scientists believe that increasing carbon dioxide levels in the atmosphere make El Niño climate changes more severe. The effects of El Niño are similar to those predicted if there is further global warming and can last for four years. The El Niño event of 1997 was the most violent of the last century. Indonesia had its worst drought for 50 years, followed by forest fires. Australia also suffered drought and bush fires.

EARLY WARNING SYSTEM

A huge chain of buoys has been placed across the tropical Pacific Ocean which automatically collect information on the ocean temperature and winds. This is fed into computers which allow scientists to give early warnings of an El Niño event.

A bush fire in the Kakadu National Park in Australia during a drought brought about by an El Niño event.

Microclimates

9

People affect the climate of large parts of the world through the air pollution they produce. They also affect the climate of smaller areas, called microclimates. Climate can vary hugely over a few metres because of differences in the wetness of the ground, the way in which it absorbs sunlight and the different types of plant cover.

A fallen forest tree creates a light, sheltered microclimate in which tree seedlings and other plants can grow.

Natural microclimates

There are millions of microclimates in the natural world. Most result from small differences in the amount of sunlight reaching the Earth's surface, or small differences in temperature, humidity or precipitation. Climate even varies at different heights in the same place. During the day, temperatures at ground level can be several degrees higher than at 2m above the ground. In hilly areas, aspect and slope affect how much the land is warmed by the Sun. In the northern hemisphere, south-facing slopes receive more Sun and less moisture than north-facing slopes. The reverse is true in the southern hemisphere.

Soil and vegetation

Microclimates also result from differences in the texture and moisture content of soils. In spring sandy soils warm up quicker than clay soils. Differences in vegetation also produce different microclimates. Inside woodland the wind speed, amount of sunlight and vertical movements of the air are less than outside. In a woodland area, it is cooler on hot days and warmer on cold evenings than outside it. Trees around a house create a microclimate by moderating the temperatures and blocking wind and sunlight. Even a tussock of grass can have its own microclimate. Lower light levels, shelter from the wind and higher humidity can provide an ideal habitat for small animals such as snails and woodlice.

Changing microclimates

Humans may deliberately change the microclimate, to provide the best conditions for growing crops or keeping livestock. Walls, fences, hedges or shelterbelts can protect growing crops from the effects of the wind. A greenhouse, cloche or polytunnel can raise the temperature and humidity of the soil and air. Farm animals can be kept in buildings where the light, heat and ventilation are carefully controlled.

People also accidentally change the microclimate of an area. The Aral Sea, on the borders of Kazakhstan and Uzbekistan in Central Asia, was once the fourth-largest inland sea in the world. It covered 68,000 sq km, but is now half that area, and more than 75 per cent of its water has evaporated.

The sea was once a natural reservoir in a vast desert and an important fishery. It began drying up in the 1960s when the two rivers that flowed into it were diverted for irrigation. This destroyed the sea's fishing industry. The Aral Sea also helped to moderate the local climate. Since the 1960s, the climate around it has changed: summers are hotter and winters colder. Every year has 150 days without rain, five times more than before.

A fishing boat stranded by the retreating waters of the Aral Sea in Central Asia.

Town and city microclimates

Wherever people make a forest clearing, build a reservoir or construct a town they create new microclimates. Towns and cities usually have higher temperatures than surrounding rural areas. Urban areas generate heat through industries, vehicles, fires, heating systems in buildings and the mass of human bodies.

Pollutants produced by industries form a layer over some cities, and at night this traps the heat in the city. Temperatures remain higher between tall buildings for longer because heat is reflected back and forth between the buildings, and the large areas of tarmac, bricks and tiles absorb more of the Sun's heat than the vegetation in the countryside. So the temperature in the centre of the biggest cities can be 10°C higher than in the surrounding countryside.

Rain, wind and smog

Cities also have an effect on local precipitation. Higher temperatures mean that there is more rising air. This, and the large quantities of dust and pollution particles in the air over a city, produces between 5 and 10 per cent more rain or other precipitation. The rainfall often falls in heavier thunderstorms during summer.

Skyscrapers and other tall buildings can act as funnels, increasing wind speed in some areas of large cities. But wind speeds are usually lower in cities than outside, because the buildings create a barrier that lowers the wind speed at ground level. These calmer conditions can lead to the build-up of photochemical smog in summer and increase the likelihood of fog in winter. The smog combined with the higher temperatures often makes the summer heat more oppressive in cities.

The high walls of these skyscrapers in Chicago, USA, act as funnels, increasing the wind speed and intensity.

Caring for our world

10

Global warming, acid rain and the hole in the ozone layer
are worldwide problems. They can be remedied only if
nations work together. Even if nations agree, there are no
easy solutions. The root of the problem is the growing world
population and the divide between rich and poor nations.

A solar-powered house in Freiburg, Germany, built in 1992. It has a wall of transparent insulation on the south side for direct heating by the Sun (passive solar heating). It heats water with solar collectors and uses solar panels to generate electricity.

Energy and fossil fuels

The high standard of living in richer countries of the world depends on industry, transport and a good supply of energy, all of which contribute to pollution. Poorer nations want to enjoy the same standard of living, but this could lead to an increase in pollution. Many of the harmful changes to our climate are the result of our reliance on fossil fuels and our wasteful use of energy. Unless we limit the output of greenhouse gases and ozone-destroying chemicals our world will become less hospitable. Continued climate change could result in millions having to be resettled because of floods, droughts or famines. We urgently need other sources of energy which do not rely on burning fossil fuels.

Alternative power sources

Nuclear power stations do not produce carbon dioxide or add to global warming. Their problems are the risk of radiation leaks and the safe disposal of nuclear waste. Solar panels trap light energy from the Sun and use it to heat water or generate electricity, so preventing much pollution. They are expensive, but once they are installed they need little attention and last for years. Their biggest drawback is that no energy is generated when the Sun is behind clouds, or at night.

Wind power, like water and solar power, is a sustainable form of energy that does not produce greenhouse gases or other air pollution. However, modern wind turbines are expensive and can be damaged by storms. They can also be noisy and a danger to wildlife.

Water power

About 17 per cent of electricity used today is generated by flowing water. The water is held back in a reservoir by a dam and piped down hill to drive turbines. These turn the generators that produce electricity. This hydroelectric power is clean, but dams are expensive and they cause problems for water life. Salmon cannot migrate up rivers to breed if dams block their route. A reservoir can provide water for domestic use, for irrigating crops and for fisheries and leisure activities. But it floods farmland and people's homes.

A hydroelectric power plant on the Hoover Dam, built on the Colorado River in the United States. About 17 per cent of the world's electricity is generated by flowing water.

The oceans and seas are underused as a source of non-polluting power. There are only two major tidal power stations: one across the River Rance in northern France and one at Annapolis Royal in Nova Scotia, Canada. A tidal power station, or barrage, is built across an estuary. As the tide flows into the river the turbines turn, generating electricity. When the tide goes out, the turbines turn in the other direction, and generate more electricity. However, tidal power stations are expensive. They can also damage wildlife and fisheries.

The waves that break on the shore contain huge amounts of energy, but this has only been harnessed in small-scale trials.

Geothermal energy

In some places heat generated inside the Earth flows near the surface, producing hot springs, geysers and boiling mud pots. Groundwater in contact with the hot rocks underground is heated, but because it is under pressure, the boiling point of the water is raised above normal and it becomes superheated. Many hot springs in Japan, New Zealand, Iceland, the United States, Mexico and other countries are harnessed to drive generators that produce electricity or to provide hot water for domestic use. However, because hot springs and geysers occur in volcano and earthquake zones, there is a danger that the pipes carrying the hot water or steam may break during an eruption or earthquake.

Biomass as fuel

In developing countries, burning biomass – plant and animal matter – generates a small but significant amount of electricity. In the developed world we hardly use biomass. This is changing, and in eastern England there are power stations that burn mainly chicken manure or straw. In Brazil, sugar cane is fermented to make alcohol, used as fuel for vehicles. In Britain there is increasing use of liquid motor fuels made from plant materials such as cereals, oilseeds and sugar beet. Recycled vegetable oils and fats can also be used instead of diesel. All these biofuels emit 50-60 per cent less carbon dioxide than fossil fuels.

Fuels from waste materials

Methane can also be a valuable fuel. Natural gas is largely methane. This gas is given off as organic matter decays when bacteria and other microbes attack it. It is a waste product of landfill sites and a potential fire risk, but it is collected in some places for fuel. Methane is also produced in warm countries where matter decays quickly. Plant remains, animal waste, left-over food and other organic materials are sealed in a container called a biodigester. As they decay, the methane produced can be used for fuel, and the rotted material for fertilizer.

Incineration

Rather than burying waste materials, some large towns and cities burn it in power stations to produce steam to turn turbines and electrical generators. The waste may contain plastics and other materials that can release toxic chemicals into the atmosphere, so the waste gases must be cleaned. The most efficient and least damaging way to dispose of domestic waste is to recycle or compost the materials it contains.

A power station in Hawaii which burns dried sugar cane stalks after the sugary juice has been extracted. This produces the steam that drives its turbines and generators.

Greener transport systems

Someone travelling by bus or train produces about 100 times less air pollution than a lone car driver. Electric trains, trams and monorails do not emit exhaust gases. But they still rely on electricity from power stations. Many cities encourage people to cycle, or to share car journeys. This reduces pollution and offers healthy exercise. Car makers are also developing lighter vehicles with more efficient engines which produce less pollution.

Electric trains such as the driverless sky train in Vancouver, Canada, reduce traffic congestion, noise and air pollution.

The importance of trees

The environment suffers in two ways when we burn trees to make way for farms, factories and roads. The trees' ability to absorb carbon dioxide is lost. Burning the wood also releases carbon dioxide which may have been locked up for years. Many people are keen to plant more trees. We could also improve our use of timber. The more we use in furniture and building, the more carbon we lock away. If trees are left to die, they rot and release carbon dioxide. We help the environment only if we replant at least as many trees as we cut down (sustainable forestry). If we eventually use the wood as fuel, the carbon dioxide given off is balanced by the amount the replacement trees take up.

WHAT CAN WE DO?

◐ Taking care of the natural environment can seem daunting. But every one of us can make a number of small decisions that will help to reduce the effect of climate change and other pollution-related problems.

◐ We can choose clean and renewable energy options, such as wind, water or solar power, when they are available.

◐ We can walk, cycle or use public transport, rather than use polluting cars, particularly for short journeys.

◐ We can reduce, reuse or recycle materials whenever possible, particularly paper.

◐ We can insulate our homes and not waste electricity. Something as simple as switching off the light when leaving a room, or not leaving a television set, computer, stereo, video or DVD player on standby can make a difference.

◐ We can avoid buying items that have unnecessary packaging.

◐ We can use energy-efficient, fluorescent light bulbs, instead of conventional light bulbs. These not only save energy and reduce pollution, they also save money.

◐ We can use water more carefully. Turning off the tap while cleaning your teeth saves about ten litres of water a day. If everyone in Britain did that they would save nearly 600 million litres of water a day. All the water we use comes originally from rain. The more water we use, the less there is to flow down streams and rivers where it keeps freshwater life in good condition and also dilutes acid rain and other pollutants.

◐ We can try to buy locally produced food. This may cost a little more, but if we buy it whenever we can, we reduce the pollution and burning of fossil fuels involved in transporting imported food.

◐ Even relatively small changes to our lifestyles can reduce the quantity of greenhouse gases we produce and significantly reduce the threat of global climate change.

Glossary

acid rain The name given to any form of precipitation which is more acid than usual because it contains dissolved pollutants.

air pressure The force of the air pressing down on the Earth's surface.

atmosphere The blanket of gases around a planet, held there by the pull of the planet's gravity.

biomass Any organic (human, animal or plant) matter that can be used as a fuel, eg wood and dung

carbon dioxide The gas produced when anything containing carbon is burned in our atmosphere. All living things and their dead remains contain carbon and all living things produce carbon dioxide when they respire.

climate The average weather in a place over a long period of time.

clouds Masses of water droplets or ice particles floating in the atmosphere. There are ten types of cloud, with three basic groups: stratus, cumulus and cirrus.

condensation The process by which a vapour or gas changes into a liquid as it cools.

Continental drift The slow movement of the continents around the globe because of forces deep inside the Earth.

Coriolis effect The way that the direction of winds is turned by the spin of the Earth – to the right in the northern hemisphere and to the left in the southern hemisphere. The Coriolis force is strongest at the poles, weakening towards the Equator, where it disappears altogether.

current A body of air or water moving in a definite direction.

deforestation The permanent removal of forests.

drought A long period of dry weather, with no rainfall.

evaporation The process by which a liquid is changed into a vapour or gas when it is heated.

fossil fuel A fuel such as coal, oil or natural gas, produced by the fossilization of decaying organic matter millions of years old.

fuel Any substance that provides energy when burnt.

global warming The warming of the Earth's atmosphere as a result of air pollution.

greenhouse effect The warming of the Earth, caused by certain gases in the atmosphere, called greenhouse gases. These allow the Sun's rays to reach the Earth's surface, but trap heat given off by the ground.

greenhouse gases Carbon dioxide, nitrous oxide, methane, ozone and CFCs that prevent heat escaping from the atmosphere into space. Without them the Earth would be too cold for living things to survive. If there is too much of them the Earth will be too hot.

humidity The amount of water vapour in the air.

hurricane A violent tropical storm in the Caribbean and North Atlantic, with winds blowing at 120 km/h or more around a low pressure centre. It is called a typhoon in the north-western Pacific and a cyclone in the Indian Ocean and around Australia.

Ice Age One of several periods in the Earth's history when huge glaciers and ice sheets covered large parts of the land surface.

meteorite The remains of a large meteor (a small piece of matter that travels round the Sun) which have not been burned up as the meteor falls through the Earth's atmosphere. They fall to Earth as a mass of metal or stone.

meteorology The study of how the atmosphere creates the weather and climate.

monsoon A wind which blows from different directions at different times of the year, causing wet and dry seasons, particularly in southern Asia, northern Australia and western Africa.

plate One of the sections of the Earth's crust. The slow but steady movements of the plates cause changes in the Earth's surface.

precipitation Any form of water (solid or liquid) that falls from the atmosphere and reaches the ground.

prevailing wind The main direction from which the wind blows in particular places.

rain shadow An area of decreased rainfall on the lee, or sheltered, side of a hill or mountain.

recycling Reusing materials or repairing an object.

relative humidity The ratio between the actual amount of water vapour in the air and the maximum amount it can hold at a given temperature.

relief rainfall Rainfall resulting from hills and mountains causing clouds to rise and cool.

renewable source of energy An unlimited source of energy, such as wind, water or wave power.

satellite A moon or spacecraft that moves in an orbit around a planet.

sediment Rock debris, such as sand, silt, mud or gravel, which is moved around by wind, water or ice.

snow-line The lowest level on a mountain above which snow never completely disappears.

solar panels Special panels that convert sunlight energy into electricity or heat.

solar power Energy from the Sun.

strata Layers of rock.

stratosphere The layer of the atmosphere that lies above the troposphere.

sustainable Something which can be maintained or kept going continuously.

temperature A measure of how hot or cold something is.

trade winds Steady winds in the tropics blowing from the north-east in the northern hemisphere and from the south-east in the southern hemisphere.

tree-line The upper limit of tree growth on a mountain.

troposphere The layer of the atmosphere that lies closest to the Earth.

water cycle The continuous circulation of water from the Earth's surface to the atmosphere, involving evaporation, condensation and precipitation.

water vapour Water in the form of an invisible gas.

weather What is happening in the atmosphere at any particular time and place in terms of clouds, humidity, sunshine, temperature, visibility, precipitation, air pressure and wind.

Index